30 Build-Your-Own BIRDHOUSES

30 Build-Your-Own BIRDHOUSES

Create delightful projects to turn your garden into a home for birds

Mary Maguire

LORENZ BOOKS

For Liz and Rob, who helped me create my own home.

This edition is published by Lorenz Books,
an imprint of Anness Publishing Ltd, Blaby Road,
Wigston, Leicestershire LE18 4SE; info@anness.com

www.lorenzbooks.com; www.annesspublishing.com

If you like the images in this book and would like to investigate
using them for publishing, promotions or advertising, please visit
our website www.practicalpictures.com for more information.

© Anness Publishing Ltd 2013

PUBLISHER'S NOTE
Although the advice and information in this book are believed to be
accurate and true at the time of going to press, neither the authors
nor the publisher can accept any legal responsibility or liability for
any errors or omissions that may have been made nor for any
inaccuracies nor for any loss, harm or injury that comes about from
following instructions or advice in this book.

Publisher: Joanna Lorenz
Editors: Margaret Malone, Anne Hildyard
Photography: Peter Williams
Designer: Nigel Partridge
Illustrator: Lucinda Ganderton
Hand model: Rupert Skinner
Production controller: Mai-Ling Collyer

Contents

Introduction

Whether your garden or back yard is in the countryside, a town or a city, it can play an important part in the conservation of wildlife, and especially of birds. As farming becomes more intensified, and more and more of the countryside is swallowed up by new housing and industrial developments, the natural habitats of many bird species are being reduced or even lost. Gardens are now more essential for their survival than ever before.

The average garden is regularly visited by 15–20 species of birds, with occasional visits from ten less common species. By simply erecting a birdtable and nesting box, you will not only be offering nature a helping hand, you will also be providing yourself with hours of interest and entertainment, and your helpful garden friends will return the favour by controlling pests, such as aphids, slugs and snails, that threaten your flower beds and vegetable patch.

Birdhouses are a charming addition to a garden. They help to ornament and personalize it, and give an even greater satisfaction if you have made them yourself. The projects in this book range from simple decorated boxes to elaborate houses. There are also creative ideas for feeders and a birdbath, with something to suit every garden and every level of experience. There are also tips on maintaining birdhouses, where and when to site them and how to keep visiting birds safe from predators.

It is pure joy when you see a bird starting to build its new home in a nesting box that you have made. From the anticipation you feel while waiting to know if the eggs have been laid and when they will hatch, to the pleasant surprise when you see the parents carrying food back to the nest, followed by the careful watching and waiting for the fledglings to emerge and gradually learn to fly, the whole experience is an exciting and rewarding one.

This book shows you how, with a little thought, you can increase the number and variety of birds that visit your garden. It offers tips on what to feed and when, and how to plan your garden with birds in mind, with planting suggestions to help you to achieve an ideal home for your feathered friends.

Creating a haven for birds is a satisfying activity. The projects in this book are practical and beautiful solutions for providing food, drink and shelter for birds.

Above: Even in an urban garden, birds will find many nooks and crannies suitable for resting, eating and nesting. Just a little planning will ensure that your garden is a welcoming haven for many types of birds.

Feathered friends

Below: Thatched bird tables have a charming rustic appeal as well as being functional tables – even if the birds do occasionally rob the thatch to build their nests!

Birds have always lived around people, and as human settlements developed, they were happy to move into them where they found cosy roosts in buildings and plenty of scraps of food. The art of domesticating wild birds has a long history, though in the early days this was generally because they were seen as a productive food source rather than for any aesthetic reason. Pigeons were probably the first birds to be domesticated, because they were good to eat, their food requirements were simple and they were prolific breeders. Both the Egyptians and the Romans built towers for them on their rooftops, fitted with internal ledges on which the birds could roost and nest.

The Native Americans had a different reason for inviting wild birds to share their homes. They used bottle-shaped gourds to make nesting boxes for purple martins, whose massed presence helped to deter vultures from raiding the meat left out to dry in the sun. Nesting boxes made from gourds are still used in North America today, and east of the Rocky Mountains the entire purple martin population lives in sites provided by humans.

It was not until fairly recent times that people began to encourage birds into their gardens purely for the joy of watching them. Gilbert White noted in his diary for June of 1782 that his brother Thomas had nailed up scallop shells under the eaves of his house, with the hollow side facing upwards against the wall, for house martins to nest in. This strategy proved very successful, as the martins began to move in almost immediately.

In the early 19th century, the pioneering naturalist Charles Waterton, who turned his estate in Yorkshire, England into a nature reserve, developed stone nesting boxes for barn owls and built a tower for jackdaws, similar to a garden dovecote.

Baron von Berlepsch was an early popularizer of nesting boxes in Britain. During the late 19th century he spent much time experimenting, eventually originating a design that replicated a natural woodpecker's nest, consisting of a section of tree trunk that had been hollowed out at one end, an entry hole that went into this chamber from the front, and a wooden lid with an attachment for fixing at the back. This simple rustic design was effective, and similar nesting boxes are still used today.

Since then, designs for nesting boxes and birdhouses have burgeoned, ranging from purely functional structures to ornate miniature versions of their owners' homes.

Creating a haven for birds

If you wish to make your garden a haven for wild birds, it's a good idea to take the birds' needs into account throughout the planning and planting process. A long-established garden or back yard, with mature trees, flowering plants and a diverse selection of shrubs, surrounded by a thick hedge, is ideal, and if your house is old it probably has nooks and crannies in its walls for roosting. Not everyone is lucky enough to have such perfect conditions, but if you are considering making some changes, it is often not difficult to improve on what you have.

CHOOSING PLANTS
You need varied vegetation that will attract insects, which will be needed once the birds are nesting. The best plants are ones that will produce plenty of nuts, berries and seeds. Birds need cover for protection, so hedges are perfect. Hawthorn is a good basic choice, as it gives dense cover for shelter from wind and rain, and for nesting. It grows quickly, and in the autumn its scarlet berries make fine pickings. If possible, keep an area of your garden wild. If you can find room for a tree, plant a native species that the birds are

adapted to. Elder produces luscious purple berries which are enjoyed by dozens of species, and a fruit tree such as apple or pear will benefit both you and the birds. Many border plants attract bees, butterflies and moths, which the birds feed on in the summer, as well as providing seeds in the autumn. Good choices include cornflowers, Michaelmas daisies, evening primroses, poppies, snap-dragons and, best of all, sunflowers, whose oil-rich seeds are irresistible to nuthatches and finches. A lawn is ideal for observation. Water the grass regularly in dry weather to bring the worms to the surface. Let it grow long around trees – the weeds will provide seed for finches.

CITY GARDENS
An urban garden may not get as great a variety of visitors as a rural one, but it has advantages. The city air is warmer so there is less threat of frost, and street lighting allows birds to feed for longer. Town or city birds are used to co-existing with people, so will tolerate closer observation. House sparrows and pigeons have adapted best to city life, but many other interesting species are attracted there too.

Above left and right: There may be many natural possibilities already in your garden that, with a little thought, can be turned into good nest sites. Choose sites that are protected from prevailing winds, rain and too much sun.

Birdwatching at home

Above: The simplest way to attract birds to your garden is to put out food for them, particularly during the winter months when natural food becomes scarce.

The variety of birds that will be attracted to your garden is influenced by your geographical position and the nature of the countryside – or lack of it – around you. In Europe and the UK, you can expect the blackbird, house sparrow, blue tit, robin, chaffinch, greenfinch, magpie, tree sparrow, collared dove, wren and dunnock, while in the US hummingbirds and goldfinches will also visit gardens.

Migration makes for interesting changes. At the end of winter some regulars will return to the countryside or migrate to more suitable breeding grounds. You may notice the odd bird that has never alighted in your garden before: it may be looking for food to fuel its long journey, or it may have been swept off course. In the winter there will be visitors looking for food, but during spring the battle for territory will begin, limiting the number of birds in your garden.

ESTABLISHING TERRITORY

A bird's territory is a fixed area that it will defend for either feeding or breeding or both. If a bird does not manage to establish its territory it will be unable to nest or breed, and may even die of hunger. The gestures birds make to communicate with each other are known as "displays". To show aggression, a bird will puff up its feathers, raise its wings and point its beak at its rival to look menacing. To show submission, a bird will crouch down and sleek its feathers in. Fights most commonly occur when a newcomer arrives in the territory of an established group, and the stranger's status needs to be evaluated. Occasionally, birds will fight to the death over a disputed area.

DAILY RITUALS

Birds wake up just before dawn, when they sing with great gusto. This dawn chorus involves many different species and lasts about half an hour, heralding the daylight. Breakfast is the best time to observe birds' behaviour, as they often quarrel over food. You will soon start to notice their pecking order. The first birds to visit the garden are likely to be blackbirds and thrushes, who come to scan the lawn in search of worms and soft grubs. They hunt quietly and carefully, pausing between hops and watching for their prey. Starlings, who arrive later, appear to stab here and there at the ground until they find a tasty morsel.

Birds have two important daily activities. The first is to find and eat food, which is done throughout the day; the second is to take care of their feathers. These must be kept in perfect condition for both flight and insulation. After bathing comes preening. Birds collect fatty oil from the preen gland at their rump and smear it over the feathers before stroking them back into place.

FINDING A PARTNER

There are three main annual events in the life of a bird: breeding, moulting and, for some, migration. Courtship generally starts in early spring (although this is weather-dependent). At the beginning of spring you may notice that the females show a pink colour at the base of their beaks, whereas the males show blue-grey. A bird may find a suitable partner by instantaneous attraction, or the process may take up to a week. Once established, the couples are often inseparable; they feed and roost together, the male guarding his mate from any rivals. The male often provides the female with food while the nest is being prepared, but it is she who usually chooses the site and builds the nest, often with her mate's help (except in the case of the wren, when it is built solely by the male).

BUILDING THE NEST
Home-making requires a lot of energy and can take as long as a month. Each species has its own specific style of construction and, once you are familiar with these, you can identify the owners.

The most common building materials are twigs, mud, pine needles, moss, dried grasses, feathers and often litter. Once completed, the nest remains empty while the female recuperates before she begins to lay her eggs. During this time, the female sheds feathers from her breast to expose a bare patch of skin which is rich with blood vessels. This is called a brood pad, and acts like a hot water bottle for incubating the eggs.

RAISING A FAMILY
The eggs are laid at 24-hour intervals until the clutch is completed. During this time the female needs to take regular feeding and bathroom breaks, and the eggs need to be regularly turned and re-arranged to keep them equally and evenly warm. In some species (including starlings, woodpeckers and swifts) the male shares incubation, developing a brood pad like his partner.

Hatching takes a few days. It starts with the chick pushing its bill into the air sack at the blunt end of the shell to begin breathing. After this comes an activity called pipping, when the chick hammers a ring of small holes in the shell which allows it to force off a section called the cap. Be patient: do not inspect the nest when waiting for the eggs to hatch. Some birds can become aggressive at this stage.

Once all the eggs are hatched, the nestlings need to be kept warm and fed. The volume of food needed will increase, and you should also cater for the dietary needs of the chicks. Their diet consists mainly of insects, worms and spiders.

LEAVING THE NEST
By the time they have grown their feathers, the young are almost too big for the nest. The fledglings must now learn to fly. For the first few days after leaving the nest, they mostly rest in a safe place, waiting for

their parents to bring food. Once they become more confident they will follow their parents. Flying is instinctive, but it often needs encouragement. Perfecting the art of flying takes practice, but the subtle wing movements are inherent.

MOULTING
Once the bird is fully grown, it needs to replace its feathers annually (or, in some species, twice yearly). Moulting ensures that damaged or worn feathers can be shed and replaced regularly and happens gradually at the end of the breeding season. It can be a stressful time because the bird has to use more energy when flying, both to keep warm and to make its new feathers. The feathers all need to be in place before winter and migration.

MIGRATION
When a bird changes its home, whatever the distance, it is said to migrate. It may only be a case of moving to a nearby city garden in the winter because the bird's summer haunt in the woods does not provide enough food, as tits do. In the case of long-distance migration, birds such as swallows, swifts and martins gather together in their particular flock and leave at the end of summer for the far shores of another, warmer, country.

Below: Though wonderful to watch, fledglings must learn to survive, so any human intervention is not a good idea.

Attracting birds

Seeing birds regularly visiting your garden (yard) is enormously rewarding. There are a few very simple ways of ensuring that your garden is attractive to birds.

BIRD TABLES
A bird table is the most obvious and effortless way to attract birds into your garden, and winter is the best time to set one up, when the natural food supply is scarce and the ground too hard for the birds to penetrate with their beaks.

Below: Ideally, feed twice a day in winter – once in the early morning and again in the early afternoon.

Your bird table may be supported on a post or brackets or it may hang from a branch. It needs a roof to keep the rain off and a rim to prevent the food from being blown away. Other additions, such as a scrap basket, seed tube or water port, may be incorporated into the design.

FEEDERS
Pet and garden suppliers stock a huge range of feeders for different types of nuts or seeds. These are useful, since seeds are easily scattered and blown away. Some are squirrel-proof. Mesh feeders are designed to dispense nuts, and those made of plastic tubing are for seeds. Instead of buying feeders, you could try making your own: there are several ideas for inexpensive versions in this book. There are also feeders that are designed to be stuck on to a window, and provided you don't mind the birds making a mess of your window and walls, these enable you to study your visitors at close proximity.

NESTING BOXES
Simple nesting boxes are generally made to hang from a tree or wall. Ready-made boxes may be plain wood, preserved with creosote, or rustic-looking hollowed-out logs fitted with roofs. It is best to choose a box that is species-specific. The all-important factor is the size of the entry hole.

If you are building your own nesting box, wood is probably the best material, though if it is thinner than 15mm/⅝in it may warp and won't offer much insulation. Old floorboards are a good source of timber, as they are well seasoned. Although softwood is easier to work with, hardwood such as oak is longer lasting. Exterior or marine plywood can be used in any situation.

Wherever possible, use the wood with the grain running vertically. This will help the rain to drain off. Glue all joints before screwing them together, or use galvanized nails, which are better for damp conditions as they will not rust easily.

Birds don't need perches on the outside of their boxes: these may cause danger, as they give predators a foothold, so avoid them.

The most important thing is that the box should be warm and dry, but not so airtight that condensation becomes a problem. There is still plenty of room for improvement with traditional designs and materials, so feel free to experiment.

BIRDHOUSES

These are ornamental versions of the nesting box. They have a dual purpose, providing a safe nesting site for birds while also satisfying our aesthetic need to decorate the garden. Designs ranging from the tasteless to the beautiful are available from garden and pet stores, and are usually post-mounted. The important thing to check when buying a birdhouse is that it will fulfil the requirements of the type of birds you want to attract. Each project indicates the typical inhabitants that it is designed for, though you need to also consider local breeds.

ROOSTS

Most birds sleep at night, with their beaks tucked under one shoulder, their heads tucked in and their feathers puffed up to keep them warm. They need regular roosting places that are protected from the elements and from predators. Birds will often use nesting boxes for this purpose, so don't despair if your house or box has not been selected for a nest site – it is still probably being used as a roost or shelter, so it's doing an important job, and possibly saving birds' lives in severe weather conditions.

BIRDBATHS

Birds get most of the water that they require from their food, but they still need to supplement this. Seed eaters, for example, need plenty of drinking water to compensate for the lack of moisture in their diet. Most drink by dipping their beaks into the water, then tilting their heads back, though pigeons are able to suck water up through their bills. Because birds don't sweat, they need another way to keep cool: they lose moisture by opening their mouths and panting.

The main purpose of providing water for birds is not for drinking but for bathing. They need to keep their feathers in good condition for both flight and insulation, and baths are just as important in winter as in summer. If their plumage is not properly maintained they will not survive the cold winter nights, so in frosty weather, it is vital to check daily

that your birdbath has not frozen over. A design for a birdbath with an ingenious anti-freezing device is included in this book. Never put antifreeze or salt into the water, as this can kill birds.

Place your birdbath in the shade. If it is in an open place, there should be cover close at hand for safety. The bath must have gently sloping sides to make it easy for small birds to use, but it should be deep enough in the middle to allow a blackbird or pigeon a full dunk. Because it will have no oxygenating plants, algae will quickly form and make the water smell unless the bath is regularly cleaned out. Do this daily in hot weather, when adding fresh water. If your birdbath has a smooth surface, put some sand or gravel in it to give the birds a secure footing, and place a large stone in the middle for them to alight on. Fountains or dripping water make baths more enticing to birds as well as appealing to human visitors.

Above: These cosy woven roosts provide a place for birds to sleep or shelter from inclement weather. They are inexpensive and look the part tucked between branches on a tree.

Left: Birds need regular bathing to keep their feathers in good condition. During winter, break any ice regularly and never put anti-freeze into the water.

Taking care of birds

Birds will quickly come to depend on your support, so once you have enticed them into the garden (yard), you need to make sure that they continue to thrive. Maintain supplies of food and water throughout the winter.

SITING AND MAINTAINING A BIRDHOUSE

When choosing sites for your birdhouse and other accessories, there are several points to bear in mind. Will they be left in peace there? It's not a good idea to erect a table, nesting box or birdbath where children play or where the pet cat tends to prowl. Birds must have shelter nearby to which to flee if danger threatens.

Place nesting boxes so that they are protected from the prevailing wind, rain and strong sunlight. If you put a box on a tree, notice which side has more algae growing. This will be the wet side, so place the box on the opposite one. If you angle the box slightly forward it will give more shelter. Be careful not to damage the tree by banging nails into it; special securing devices are available for this

Below: Be restrained when setting up your garden. One or two boxes in an average-sized garden is enough. Any more than that will cause distress.

purpose. Boxes don't have to be rigidly mounted, as long as they are secure. Boxes that hang from a wire or string work well and they may offer better protection from predators.

The best time of year to put up nesting boxes is in the autumn. They can then act as roosts during the winter and be ready for early spring when the birds start choosing their breeding grounds. During the winter you can insulate them with cotton, straw or wood shavings for roosting birds, but remember to remove this padding before nesting begins in the spring. Don't overdo the number of boxes you set up in your garden. Robins and tits can be very territorial and aggressive with their own species.

Cleaning out the houses and nesting boxes after the breeding season is very important. Wash them out with diluted mild disinfectant, wearing rubber gloves to protect you from parasites.

If birds do nest in your boxes, don't be tempted to sneak a look – the shock may cause the mother to abandon her brood or the young chicks to leave their nest prematurely.

FEEDING THE BIRDS

Birds will appreciate fresh food on the table in the morning, or at least at a regular time. If you need to go away, fill up your feeder and leave fat balls to sustain the birds until your return. Birds need food with a high fat and carbohydrate content; they may lose up to 10 per cent of their body weight overnight in bad weather, so suet, cheese, bacon rinds and dripping will help them build up their energy reserves. Crows, starlings, tits and woodpeckers are attracted to bacon rind, fat and crumbled cheese.

The shape of a bird's beak roughly indicates its diet. Finches have hard, thick beaks which are designed to crack and crush. They feed mostly on grain and seed. Robins and wrens, with their slender, soft beaks, eat caterpillars, grubs and other insects. Gulls, starlings and blackbirds have general-purpose bills, which allow them to eat a bit of everything. Whatever the species, they enjoy culinary variety, and kitchen scraps are welcome on the bird table. Bread is the food most commonly put out for birds, but it is not very good for them. If you do give it, soak it in water or, even better, fat. In fact any dried foods – especially fruits – should be soaked. Never give birds desiccated (dry, shredded) coconut or uncooked rice. These swell up in their stomachs and can kill. Kitchen leftovers such as baked potatoes and spaghetti are good: they are soft enough for the birds to eat but difficult for them to pick up whole to fly away with. Keep some of your windfall apples and pears in storage until winter, when they will be welcome cut up on the bird table.

Pet stores sell a variety of ready-mixed birdseed, or you can make your own mixture, using grains such as millet, sunflower, hemp, niger, popping corn, wheat grain and barley. Nuts are also popular. Those with hard shells are best cracked open. Peanuts in their shells can be strung on thread or wire (don't use multistranded thread as birds may get their feet caught in this). Ensure the nuts are fresh – mouldy ones produce a toxin that kills many garden birds.

Half a coconut hanging on a string offers good value for money and provides delightful entertainment when acrobatic tits come to feed. Once its flesh has been stripped, the shell can be filled with wholesome bird pudding, a mixture of nuts, seeds and melted fat. Place feeders in the open, not overhung by trees, or birds may be reluctant to feed, because of the risk of being ambushed by cats. It is important to keep your bird table clean so that droppings don't accumulate, as this can cause bacterial infection. Always remove any uneaten food before it goes mouldy. Don't worry if birds don't visit your feeder immediately – it may take up to two weeks for a bird table to be accepted by the neighbourhood birds.

PROTECTING BIRDS

A bird's life is full of hazards, so much so that most birds die young. The average life expectancy for an adult songbird is just two years. It is not only the winter that is perilous; summer claims as many lives and breeding time is as dangerous as migration.

If you are going to encourage birds into your garden, it is your duty to protect them, especially from cats. If you do have a cat, put a bell on its collar to alert the birds to its presence, or keep it in while the birds are at their morning feed. Make sure nesting boxes are sited in places cats cannot reach. You can put chicken wire around a box, as long as

there is room for the birds to get in and out. Food left on the ground encourages rats, who will take every opportunity to steal and eat birds' eggs. Grey squirrels will also do this. They will even gnaw around the entrance hole of a nesting box to make it bigger in order to steal the nestlings. They are also a menace on bird tables and feeders. Mounting your tables and houses on smooth, slippery posts will prevent cats, squirrels and rats from clambering up.

Tree-mounted boxes can have smooth protective collars of plastic projecting from the entrance hole, or be mounted on a slippery backplate. An internal ledge under the entrance hole of the box ensures that the nestling can hide should a predator trespass.

Several organizations are involved with the protection and conservation of wild birds, and all will answer enquiries. Contact local groups for information on birds in your area. We can all help to ensure that these remarkable creatures survive in all their variety, despite losses to their natural habitats.

Above: Mount boxes far enough up trees so that there is no danger of animals, such as cats, reaching the box, especially when there is an outside ledge attached to the box.

Building materials

Cosy nests for garden birds can be constructed using a wide variety of materials, even a hollowed-out log. The garden shed will probably provide many suitable materials, such as sticks, string, garden wire, and offcuts (scraps) of wood.

ALUMINIUM MESH
Useful for making bird feeders, this is available from hardware stores and some hobby suppliers. Birds can peck food through a coarse mesh, while a fine gauze can be used to line the base of a feeder to enable rain to drain away.

CLAY
A birdhouse moulded from potter's clay will need to be fired in a kiln. Self-hardening clay does not need firing, and is available in various colours, including stone and terracotta. Varnish the clay to make it water resistant.

COCONUT
Birds love fresh coconut, and when they have eaten the contents you can use the half shells as parts of a birdhouse or fill them with bird pudding. Never put out dessicated (dry, shredded) coconut.

CORRUGATED ROOFING MATERIAL
An offcut or scrap from a DIY or hardware store would cover a large birdhouse. You will need special screws to attach it.

HANGING BASKET LINERS
Basket liners are available in a soft green with a texture resembling moss. They can be cut to size and moulded over chicken wire.

PAINT AND VARNISH
Use exterior quality paint with a satin or matt finish. If you use emulsion (latex) paint, it will need to be protected with a varnish designed for exterior use, such as yacht varnish. For fine work, use craft enamels or artist's acrylics.

PAINTBRUSHES
You will need a range of small household paintbrushes, together with medium and fine artist's brushes for detailed decoration. Clean brushes in white spirit (turpentine) if you are using oil-based paints.

PALETTE
Use a white ceramic tile or an old plate to mix paint colours.

READY-MADE BIRDHOUSES
Buy these inexpensively and customize them to suit your garden.

ROOFING SLATES AND TILES
Beautiful old roofing slates and tiles can be bought from salvage yards and make excellent weatherproof roofs for birdhouses.

SELF-ADHESIVE ROOF FLASHING
This material looks like lead, and is tough and waterproof for roofs.

SHELLS
These make pretty decorations on wooden houses. Gather them at the beach or you may have an old shell necklace you can recycle.

STICKS
Garden canes are easily available in a range of sizes, either bamboo or green-stained. Thick stakes can be used to support some houses. Withes are willow stems used for weaving. They are available stripped or unstripped, and become very pliable once soaked. Straight hazel twigs can be gathered in the garden or hedgerow.

STRING
Household string is useful for hanging up feeders. Green garden string and natural raffia make good binding materials and garden string has been treated for outdoor use. Sea grass string is strong.

WIRE
Plastic-coated chicken wire is attractive and will not scratch your hands. Garden wire is also plastic-coated and comes in various gauges. Galvanized wire is useful for constructing and suspending birdhouses. Florist's wire is much thinner and is useful for binding.

WOOD
For long-lasting, weatherproof houses, use timber that is at least 15mm/⅝in thick. Planed pine comes in a wide range of widths; treat it with preservative, or paint or varnish it. Tongue and groove or ship-lap boards make attractive walls for larger birdhouses. Marine or exterior quality plywood is easy to cut with a fretsaw for decorative panels and small components.

Clockwise from top left: Natural and planed wood, ready-made birdhouse, natural and treated willow, aluminium mesh and wire sheets, galvanised and plastic-coated wire, paints, paintbrushes, string, liner, roof slate, coconut, self-adhesive flashing, clay, sticks and shells.

Building equipment

No special equipment is needed for building birdhouses since only basic carpentry skills are needed. Take care when using new equipment and always check against templates before cutting.

ADHESIVES
Glue all joints in wooden birdhouses, using wood glue, before nailing or screwing them together. Masking tape can be useful for holding wood together while glue is drying. Two-part epoxy resin glue makes a strong bond when you are joining disparate materials. Small stones or shells can be embedded in ready-mixed tile cement for a decorative finish. Always use exterior grade glue, especially when working with PVA (white glue).

BROWN PAPER
Heavy craft paper makes a good protective covering for your work surface when painting or gluing. Old newspaper is also ideal as protective covering.

CRAFT KNIFE AND SCISSORS
Always use a sharp blade in a craft knife and protect the work surface with a cutting mat. When using self-adhesive flashing, cut with a sharp knife, rather than scissors.

DRILL AND BITS
For making holes for screws and other fixings (attachments). Spade bits can be used for entry holes up to 2.5cm/1in. Hole saws, which fit on to a drill, are available in a range of sizes to cut larger entry holes for birdhouses. You can also cut an entry hole with a fretsaw and jigsaw, if a hole saw is not available.

GLOVES
Gardening gloves will protect you from scratches when you are handling and bending wire. Latex gloves will keep your hands clean when you are painting or modelling clay.

HAMMER AND NAILS
Use nails that will not rust, such as galvanized nails or moulding pins that are plated.

PENCIL AND RULERS
Use a sharp pencil and ruler for accurate marking out of wood. Use a metal ruler when cutting with a craft knife.

PLIERS AND CUTTERS
Both general purpose and small, round-nosed pliers are useful for working with wire. You will also need wire cutters. Lead flashing, for roofs, can be cut using tin snips.

SANDPAPER
Smooth the edges of the wood after cutting uisng medium sandpaper wrapped around a wooden block. Roll a piece of sandpaper around your finger to smooth the edges of entry holes.

SAWS
Use a tenon saw for square cutting; for large cuts, you will need a panel saw. Curved shapes can be cut using a jigsaw. Use a fretsaw for small intricate shapes, supporting the wood on a V-board screwed to the workbench. Use a hacksaw to cut metal.

SCREWS AND SCREWDRIVER
Screws make secure fixings (attachments) in large, heavy structures. Plated pozidriv screws are less likely to rust for outdoor use.

VICE AND CLAMPS
A vice or adjustable workbench is essential for holding wood steady when you are sawing it. A bench hook is helpful when cutting timber with a tenon saw as it is good for cutting strips to length. Clamp a coconut in a vice to saw it in half. Clamps of various sizes, and even clothes pegs (pins) are useful for holding work together during assembly.

Clockwise from top left: Sandpaper and wooden blocks, panel and tenon saw, drill kit and bits, brown paper, hacksaw, paintbrushes, pencil and ruler, craft knife and masking tape, scissors, pliers and cutters, screwdriver and screws, hammers and nails, epoxy resin glue, wood glue and spatula, latex and fabric gloves and vice.

Bounty bower

In the winter, the food you provide can make the difference between life and death for some birds. Once you have started, you should continue to put food out every day, but for a real treat offer this gourmet selection. Adjust the quantities to suit the number of birds that call.

You will need

apple
skewer
garden wire
wire cutters
sunflower seeds
metal eyelets
pine cones
string
scissors
knife
millet bunches
raffia
darning needle
strong thread
unroasted monkey nuts
  (peanuts in their shells)
hacksaw
whole coconut
drill
unsalted, unroasted smooth
  peanut butter (from health
  food stores)
mixed birdseed

Typical feeders

goldfinches
hawfinches
grosbeaks

1 Skewer an apple and thread it on to a long piece of garden wire. Wind the end around the base of the apple to prevent it slipping off. Embed sunflower seeds into the flesh of the apple.

2 Screw metal eyelets into the base of a selection of pine cones. Thread them with lengths of string and tie the cones together in size order. Hang the string on an existing bower.

3 Tie a selection of millet bunches with raffia. Using a darning needle and strong thread, thread monkey nuts (peanuts) to make long strings. Saw a coconut in half. Drill two holes near the edge of one half and thread a piece of wire through them. Twist the ends of the wire together; hang them from the bower.

4 Once the birds have pecked all the seeds out of the pine cones, you can revamp them by spreading them with unsalted, unroasted smooth peanut butter then dipping each cone into a bowl of small mixed seeds. The seeds will stick to the peanut butter.

Wire bird feeder

Small aluminium cans and aluminium mesh form the basis for this simple bird feeder. Ordinary household scissors will cut through the cans, but be careful not to leave any sharp or jagged edges. They can be filled with various types of nuts, scraps and larger seeds.

1 Using old scissors, cut a small aluminium drink (soda) can in half, then draw a decorative scalloped border around each half and cut out. Trim off any jagged edges.

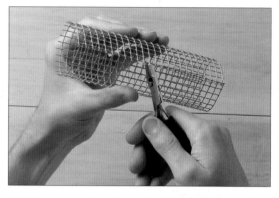

2 Cut a rectangle of mesh to fit, rolled up, inside the can. Roll the mesh around a bottle. Join the edges by hooking the cut ends through the mesh and bending them over, using pliers.

3 Use a bradawl to pierce a hole in the bottom of the can. Fit the mesh cylinder into the two halves of the can, then thread them the structure on to galvanized wire. Twist the lower end of the wire into a flat coil so that the feeder cannot slide off.

4 Leave a length of wire above the top of the can long enough for the top to slide up off the mesh, for refilling, then allow an extra 7.5cm/3in. Cut the wire. Twist the end into a flat coil, then make a hook by bending the wire over a marker pen. Repeat with the remaining cans.

A sweet treat

This prettily shaped pudding will look lovely in the garden and make feeding the birds much more fun, especially if you want to interest your children in birdwatching. You can also mould fat puddings in an empty yogurt pot, but let the mixture cool before filling.

You will need

75g/3oz lard
saucepan
shelled nuts
seeds
berries
wooden spoon
string
heart-shaped mould
raisins
dried cranberries
garden wire
wire cutters
bowl of water
ribbon

Typical feeders

starlings
tits
nuthatches
waxwings

1 Melt 75g/3oz lard in a saucepan and stir in a generous mixture of shelled peanuts and almonds, pumpkin seeds, sunflower seeds, raisins and cranberries.

2 Lay a doubled piece of string in the bottom of a mould and spoon in the mixture, embedding the string. Smooth the top of the pudding and leave it to cool.

3 Thread raisins and cranberries alternately on to garden wire long enough to surround the heart pudding. Twist the ends together and soak the wreath in water to plump up the fruit.

4 When the pudding is set, turn it out of the mould and tie the string to the twisted ends of the wire so that the heart is suspended in the middle of the wreath. Tie a ribbon over the join.

Coconut feeder

A plastic tube, made from a recycled cosmetic bottle, makes a practical seed-dispenser. The half-coconut roof lifts off to the side, allowing you to refill the plastic tube. Tits are particularly adept at using this kind of feeder and their acrobatics can be entertaining.

1 Drill two small holes in the top of each coconut and drain out the milk. From one, cut out two 5cm/2in holes on opposite sides and a third at the top. Then remove the flesh with a knife.

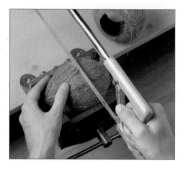

2 Using a hacksaw, cut the second coconut in half. Remove the flesh from one half to form the roof of the feeder. Make a small central hole in the top and two small holes on each side near the rim.

3 Beneath each large side hole in the first coconut, drill two tiny holes on either side. These will be used for holding the perches. Drill two further holes on each side for attaching the roof.

4 Remove the top and bottom of a plastic bottle to make a tube and cut out two semicircular shapes at the bottom on opposite sides (these will allow the seeds to spill out). Place the tube in the first coconut through the large hole at the top.

5 Attach a perch beneath each side hole by threading florist's wire through the small drilled holes and around a twig, twisting it to form a cross over the centre. Using small pliers, twist the ends of the wire together inside the coconut.

6 Attach the roof to the base by threading string through the side holes in the coconuts. Tie a bead to a doubled piece of string, to act as an anchor, and thread the string through the central hole of the roof for hanging.

Bottle feeder

This elegant and practical seed feeder keeps the contents dry. The flow of seed can be regulated by adjusting the height of the bottle, but remember to cover the opening while you insert the filled bottle into the frame, to avoid spillage.

1 Measure your chosen bottle against the metal bracket that you are going to use, and, if the bracket is too long, carefully cut off the excess metal using a hacksaw.

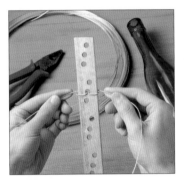

2 Cut a piece of wire long enough to wrap around the bottle in a criss-cross fashion. Thread both ends of the wire through an appropriate hole near the top of the bracket.

3 Place the bottle in position on the bracket and wrap the wire around it, forming a cross. Secure the wire through a suitable hole at the back of the bracket.

4 Repeat the process at the neck of the bottle, so that the bottle is held in place by two lots of crossed wire. Twist the ends of the wire together at the back of the bracket.

5 Remove the bottom of the tart tin (disposable pie pan) and use it as a template to cut out a circular piece of aluminium gauze. Glue the gauze into the bottom of the tin (pan).

6 Using florist's wire, attach the tin (pan) to the arm of the bracket by threading the wire through the aluminium gauze. Secure it by tying it around the bracket.

Decorating birdhouses

Inexpensive ready-made plain boxes can be customized to suit your taste. Paint makes for the simplest transformations, but you could create a grotto-like effect with shells and sea-washed glass, or a leafy hideaway using fabric shapes.

Alpine house

You will need

ready-made birdhouse
primer
paintbrushes
pencil
emulsion (latex) paints in
    duck-egg blue, rust red,
    white, grey, primrose
    yellow and pale green
matt varnish and brush

Typical inhabitant

tits

1 Prime the birdhouse and leave to dry. Draw the design on the box in pencil. Paint the roof, shutters, stonework and window-box in duck-egg blue.

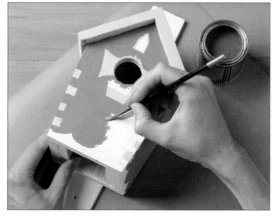

2 When the first colour is completely dry, paint the walls of the house in rust red, being careful to avoid going over the details painted in duck-egg blue.

3 Add the details on the gable and shutters in white. Outline the stonework and window box in grey. Paint the curtains and the flowers in the box primrose and the grass pale green.

4 Paint a loose arrangement of flowers along the front and sides of the birdhouse in primrose, adding pale green leaves. Once dry, coat with matt varnish.

Shaker-style house

You will need

ready-made birdhouse
primer
paintbrushes
scissors
paper and pencil
emulsion (latex) paints in
  rust red and duck-egg
  blue
self-adhesive roof flashing
craft knife and mat
matt varnish and brush

Typical inhabitant

tits

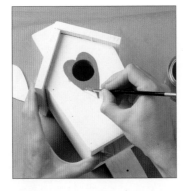

1 Prime the birdhouse and leave to dry. Cut a heart out of paper and position it over the entry hole. Draw around it in pencil and paint the heart rust red.

2 Paint the walls in duck-egg blue, taking care not to paint over the detail. When they are dry, paint on little starbursts in rust red using a very fine artist's brush.

3 Cut a piece of roof flashing to fit the birdhouse roof. Cover the roof, folding the edges neatly under the eaves. Protect the paintwork by applying matt varnish.

Leafy birdhouse

You will need

ready-made birdhouse
primer
paintbrush
emulsion (latex) paint in
  mid-blue
waterproof green canvas
scissors
staple gun
all-purpose glue
waterproofing wax spray,
  if needed

Typical inhabitants

nuthatches
wrens

1 Prime the birdhouse and leave to dry. Paint the birdhouse a colour complimentary to your canvas, such as mid-blue, and leave to dry. Cut the canvas into 4cm/1½in bands and scallop one edge. Staple the bands on to the house, starting at the base and allowing the scallops to overhang.

2 Staple more canvas bands around the front and sides of the box, each layer overlapping the last. When you reach the entry hole, snip the top of the canvas band and glue it down inside the hole. Staple on the next band, then trim back the central scallop to form a few small fronds above the entry hole.

3 Overlay strips on the side of the roof. Cut the top strip double the width, with a scalloped edge along both sides, so that it fits over the roof ridge.

4 Finally, staple bands along the gable ends. Spray the finished house with water-proofing wax, if not using a waterproof fabric.

Shell house

You will need

ready-made birdhouse
selection of seashells,
  sea-worn glass and beads
ready-mixed tile cement
palette knife (metal
  spatula)
sharp knife, if needed

Typical inhabitants

tits
sparrows

1 Choose pretty shells to overhang the eaves of the birdhouse. Spread the cement over a small area at a time and thickly enough to embed the shells firmly into it as you go.

2 Select some small shells and beads to surround the entry hole in a regular design. Continue until the front and sides of the house are completely covered with shells.

3 Use two flat scallop shells to cover each side of the sloping roof. Embed these firmly into the cement.

4 A razor shell makes a perfect ridge tile. Cut to size using a sharp knife, if necessary, and press into position with a liberal amount of cement. Remove any excess and leave until the cement is completely set.

Above: For greatest effect, use shells of varying colour, size and texture.

Clay pot roost

For this project you will need access to a kiln (perhaps through a local education centre or school), but you do not need to be skilled in pottery. Cut the entry hole to suit your choice of potential resident, and site the pot in a sheltered position.

You will need

paper
pencil
scissors
latex gloves
clay
rolling pin
craft knife
length of 10cm/4in
  diameter plastic
  plumbing pipe
brown craft paper
round cutter
bradawl
fresh leaves, to decorate
kiln

Typical inhabitants

wrens

1 From the paper, cut a circle 12cm/4½in in diameter, a rectangle 12 x 17cm/4½ x 6½in, and a semicircle 38cm/15in in diameter. Roll out the clay to 8mm/⅜in thickness and cut out the shapes. Cover the pipe in paper and roll the rectangular clay piece around it.

2 Seal the joint at the side by smoothing the overlap down with your thumb. Cut an entry hole 25mm/1in in diameter, about a third of the way down from the top, using a plain round cutter.

3 Keeping the pipe inside the clay cylinder, add the circular section to make the base, and join on to the side by smoothing the edges together. Remove the pipe.

4 Wrap the semicircle of clay into a cone and join the sides as before to make the lid of the roost.

5 Mould a small bird from some leftover clay to decorate the top of the lid. Model the wings separately and carefully mark the feathers and eyes using a bradawl.

6 Smooth clay over the base of the bird and the top of the lid to attach the bird. Fire the base and the lid separately in a kiln. To decorate, press fresh leaves into the clay before firing.

Seaside bird table

The pretty decorative details and distressed paintwork of this bird table are reminiscent of seaside architecture. You can use plain dowelling – or a broom handle – to make the supports for the roof, or recycle the turned legs from an old piece of furniture.

1 Following the templates at the back of the book, mark out the base, roof base and roof ends on the 2cm/¾in pine board. Cut out using a scroll saw or jigsaw. Drill a 2cm/¾in diameter hole in each corner of the two bases, lining them up first. Glue the roof ends to the roof base. Screw into place.

2 In the base, drill a starter hole for the fretsaw. Cut out a 7.5cm/3in diameter hole, 5cm/2in in from one short side. Sand all the surfaces. Glue the four dowelling supports in place on the frame and base. Leave to dry overnight.

3 From the 4mm/⅛in plywood, cut five strips 2.5cm/1in wide for each roof end panel, and cut to shape. Cut seven 2.5cm/1in strips for each side of the roof. Cut out the scalloped edging pieces for the roof and base, four strips for the eaves and two lozenges for the roof top ends. Sand all the surfaces.

4 Glue the plywood strips across the roof ends and nail in place with the pins. Attach the roof slats along the sides of the roof, and the scalloped frills all around the roof edge and the base. When hammering small pins, a piece of cardboard can safely hold the pin steady.

5 Paint the bird table with a dilute mixture of cobalt blue and burnt umber watercolour paints, in equal proportions. Leave to dry, then coat with a thin layer of petroleum jelly, smearing it on with your fingers. Treating one surface at a time, apply a coat of white emulsion (latex) paint and dry it with a blowtorch to make the paint crack. To paint the eaves, mix a little turquoise and yellow ochre watercolour into the emulsion.

6 To age the paintwork, apply a dilute, equal mixture of yellow ochre and burnt sienna watercolours. Leave to dry, then finish with a coat of satin yacht varnish. Attach to a ready-made stand and place a water bowl in the table.

Shanty town bird table

It is a real treat to watch birds feeding, and seeing them at close range from the comfort of your armchair is even better. This bamboo structure is designed to hang on a wall from two cup hooks. Position it near a window so that you can see the birds easily.

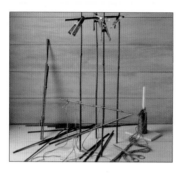

1 Mark and cut out a rectangle 12 x 16cm/4½ x 6¼in on the timber offcut (scrap). Drill a hole in each corner of the rectangle and push in four 90cm/36in canes. Cut two short lengths of cane and clip them diagonally at the top to hold the uprights in place.

2 Using the templates at the back of the book as a guide, tie on the horizontal canes, using garden string. These will hold the baking tin (pan) firmly on each side. Add two diagonal canes on each side as shown, to reinforce the structure.

3 Tie on the roof supports on each side, again using the templates given at the back of the book as a guide.

4 Join the two sides of the structure together, first by attaching the bottom diagonal canes, then with two pieces running straight across at the level of the feeding tray.

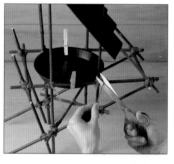

5 To attach the roof, drill four holes in the roofing sheet. Unclip the top diagonals and push the roof down over the uprights until it is resting on the roof supports. Tie on the long top diagonals.

6 Snip off the long ends of the string and attach the feeding tray with two clothes pegs (pins). Use the top long diagonals to hang food from, such as a whisk as a fat ball holder, or nuts.

Wall-mounted dovecote

This beautiful structure will make a comfortable roost for up to half a dozen doves, but it can be adapted to accommodate more birds by increasing the number of tiers. It can be sited on the side of a building or mounted on a post.

You will need

pencil
ruler
square
12mm/½in and 6mm/¼in
  plywood
jigsaw
2cm/¾in pine board
tenon saw
2 x 4.5cm/¾ x 1¾in pine
  batten
sandpaper
wood glue
nails
hammer
drill
screws
screwdriver
paint
paintbrush
self-adhesive roof flashing
craft knife
cutting mat
metal ruler

Typical inhabitant

doves

1 Using the template at the back of the book, mark and cut out the backboard from 12mm/½in plywood, using a jigsaw. Cut the roof shapes and the front arches from 6mm/¼in plywood.

2 Mark and cut out all the pine timber components from 20mm/¾in thick planks, following the templates provided. The sides and centre will require wide boards. Sand all the surfaces.

3 Join the sides and centre by gluing and nailing on the front battens. Fit the back battens into the notches cut in the centre piece. Attach by nailing at the batten's centre and from each side.

4 Drill pilot holes for the screws in the backboard. Attach the backboard to the frame using glue and screws. Paint the frame and the arched fronts and leave to dry. Attach the fronts using glue and nails.

5 Cover the small roof sections with self-adhesive roof flashing. Cover the main roof with horizontal strips of flashing. Start from the bottom of the roof and overlap each section, allowing some overlap on the final piece to attach to the backboard when assembled.

6 Using nails, assemble the final parts in the following order: first the small roof sections; then the floors; then the main roof. Attach the dovecote to a wall by screwing through the backboard from the inside. Take care when fixing, as the structure is heavy.

Little brick birdhouse

As long as a birdhouse is weatherproof and sited in a safe, sheltered position, its external appearance will not affect the inhabitants. This sturdy little house is actually made of wood faced with self-hardening clay and roofed with slate.

You will need

pencil
ruler
2cm/¾in pine board
tenon saw
drill
wood glue
nails
hammer
enamel paints
paintbrushes
paper
scissors
terracotta self-hardening
  clay
board
rolling pin
knife
epoxy resin glue
blunt-ended modelling
  tool
acrylic paints
satin exterior varnish
varnish brush
slate
face mask
hacksaw

Typical inhabitant

sparrows

1 Using the templates, cut out the birdhouse pieces from the board. Drill an entry hole in one side. Glue and nail the box together. Draw, then paint, the door and window on the front.

2 Make paper patterns of the sides and front. Cut out the entry hole, front door and window. Roll out the clay to 8mm/⅜in thick. Lay the patterns on the clay and cut around them.

3 Cover the front of the house with epoxy resin glue, taking care to avoid the painted door and window, then carefully lay the clay over the front, fitting it into the correct position.

4 Inscribe the fancy brickwork around the window and door using a blunt-ended modelling tool, then use a ruler to press in horizontal lines as a guide for the standard brickwork. Inscribe the brickwork with the modelling tool. Repeat on the side walls.

5 Paint over some of the bricks using acrylic paints to imitate the variations in real brickwork. Leave to dry completely, then coat with a satin exterior varnish.

6 Cut a piece of slate to size, wearing a protective mask. It helps to saw through each side edge before cutting right across. Drill four holes for the nails and attach the roof to the side walls of the house.

Noah's ark

Solidly constructed in pine, this miniature ark has a removable roof covered in flashing. You can tie the ark into a tree, placing it securely in the crook of some branches, or, as it has a flat base, mount it on a post.

1 Copy the templates at the back of the book on to paper and cut them out. Mark out the shapes for the hull on the 2cm/¾in pine board, fixing the paper with two pins, if necessary.

2 Using a jigsaw, cut out the outside shape of each hull section and the notches for the bow and stern.

3 Saw out the central area of each hull section, first drilling a hole in the square to take the jigsaw blade. Sand all the surfaces to make them smooth.

4 Mark out and cut out the components for the hut, using a tenon saw, and drill an entry hole in one end wall. Glue the pieces, then reinforce by nailing them together.

5 Turn the hut upside down and hold it steady in a vice, then glue and nail the top layer of the hull on to the bottom of the hut. Make sure it is centrally positioned before attaching.

6 Glue and nail the remaining layers of the hull, one at a time in order of size, using the bow and stern to align the segments. Do not glue the bow or stern into position yet.

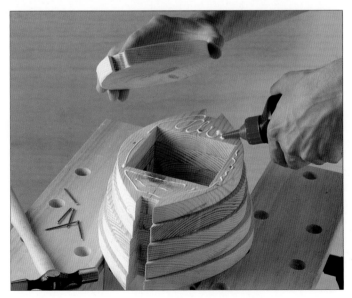

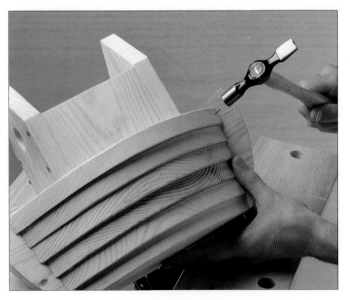

7 When all the layers of the hull are attached, glue and nail the base into position to complete the hull.

8 When the glue is completely dry, turn the hull on to its side and now glue and nail the bow and stern pieces in place.

9 To make the roof, cut out two pieces of plywood to the measurements given on the templates, and glue and nail them together as shown, using a length of pine batten to reinforce the joint.

10 Paint the hull and hut, leave to dry, then protect with a couple of coats of varnish. Cut the flashing into strips long enough to turn under the edge of the roof. Cut a scalloped edge along one side of each strip to resemble roof tiles.

11 Scallop the final piece of flashing along both edges and carefully stick it along the ridge of the roof ensuring it is even on both sides.

12 Finally, drill a hole through each end wall and into the roof ridge reinforcement, and attach the roof to the ark using two loose nails.

Blue tit nesting box

Inspired by Edwardian seaside architecture, this pretty box is designed for blue tits. Fretwork is satisfying to make, but it does require practice and patience. However, your efforts will be rewarded once you see your creation hanging on the garden wall.

1 Using the templates at the back of the book, mark out and cut out the base, back (of box), sides and lid from 2cm/¾in pine. Cut the notches in the side pieces. Plane the edges of the base and lid to line up with the sides. Cut a length of dowelling for the perch.

2 Mark out the back plate, front, the circular frame for the entry hole and the decorative panel for the lid front on 4mm/⅙in plywood and cut out using a fretsaw and V-board. Cut out a 2.5cm/1in entry hole in the front panel. Sand all the surfaces.

3 Glue the sides, base and back support together and secure with moulding pins. Glue and nail the fretwork panel to the front edge of the lid. Drill a hole for the perch below the entrance hole, and glue into place, then glue and nail the front to the sides.

4 Paint the box with a dilute mixture of cobalt blue and burnt umber watercolour paints, in equal proportions. Leave to dry, then coat with a thin layer of petroleum jelly, smearing it on with your fingers. To age the hinges, paint with tourmaline antiquing medium.

5 Treating one surface at a time, apply a coat of white emulsion (latex) paint and dry it with a blowtorch to make the paint crack. Add a little turquoise and yellow ochre watercolour to the emulsion (latex) to make pale green for the entry hole frame and backboard.

6 Glue and nail the back panel on to the box. To age the paintwork, apply a diluted, equal mixture of yellow ochre and burnt sienna watercolours until you achieve the desired effect. Leave to dry, then finish with varnish. Screw on the hinges to attach the lid.

Ridge tile retreat

This elegant birdhouse is divided into two, with an entry hole at each end, and is made to suit larger birds, such as starlings, which live in colonies. A decorative old ridge tile makes an excellent shelter and is stable enough not to need attaching to the walls.

You will need

pencil
ruler
2cm/¾in pine board
tenon saw
drill
hole saw
sandpaper
wood glue
galvanized nails
hammer
paint
paintbrush
ridge tile

Typical inhabitant

starlings

1 Using the templates, mark and cut out the components for the birdhouse, adapting the pitch of the roof to fit your tile. Drill an entry hole in each end. Sand all the surfaces.

2 Glue and nail the floor to the sides of the birdhouse, then mark the centre of the box and glue the dividing wall in position.

3 Glue and nail each gable end piece to the sides. Paint the outside of the birdhouse and leave until completely dry.

4 Place the ridge tile on the top of the birdhouse. This house can be erected on a post or simply placed at medium height in a quiet location.

Nest-in-a-boot

The boot is half-filled with gravel to stabilize it, and a small basket makes a perfect foundation for the nest. Try to find an interesting seed pod or other natural decoration for the roof. The birds won't need the little ladder, but children will love it.

You will need

rubber boot
scissors
gravel
small round basket
bradawl
string
small sticks
epoxy resin glue
wooden curtain ring
fabric gloves
chicken wire
wire cutters
small pliers
sisal hanging-basket liner
large-eyed needle
raffia
interesting seed pod
garden wire

Typical inhabitant

tits

1 Cut down the boot to a suitable size and cut out a small entry hole towards the top. Fill the bottom of the boot with gravel, then wedge a small round basket into position below the entry hole.

2 Make two small holes below the entry hole to either side. Thread a long piece of string through these and tie on little sticks to form a ladder. Glue on a wooden curtain ring over the entry hole as reinforcement.

3 To make the roof, wear protective gloves to cut a semicircular piece of chicken wire, with wire cutters, and curve it to form a cone. Using pliers, join the sides by twisting the ends of the wire together.

4 Wrap a piece of the sisal basket liner around the cone, pressing the wire rim into the matting all the way around. Turn in the edges of both matting and chicken wire.

5 Cross stitch down the join with string, then cross stitch around the bottom with raffia. Insert the seed pod decoration into the point of the roof and glue in place.

6 Make four pairs of holes, evenly spaced around the rim of the boot. Attach the roof to the boot using four lengths of garden wire and twist the wires together. Snip off excess wire.

Robin's log cabin

Designed for robins, who like open-fronted nesting boxes, this log cabin-effect box
will blend in nicely with the natural environment. Position it low down in a well-hidden site,
preferably surrounded by thorny shrubbery, well away from any other birdhouses.

1 Select evenly sized, straight
sticks and cut them to length,
using a tenon saw and bench
hook. You will need four
uprights 15cm/6in long, 10
sticks to make the base
12cm/4¾in long, and about 50
for the sides, 10cm/4in long.

2 Construct the first side by
nailing 10cm/4in lengths to
two of the uprights. Repeat to
make the other side.

3 Attach the two sides by
nailing more small sticks
across the back, from top to
bottom.

4 Turn the box over. Attach
one stick at the top of the
front, then leave a gap of about
5cm/2in before completing the
rest of the front. Use the 12cm/
4¾in sticks to make the base.

5 Build up the top of the box
by adding two more short
sticks to each side, on top of the
existing pieces.

6 Fit the tray into the top so
that it rests on the uprights.
Cut a piece of turf to fit and
place it in the tray.

Thatched birdhouse

As long as the basic box requirements are fulfilled, the finish is up to you. Tailor-made for sparrows, who will take to almost any hole, this box should be sited somewhere quiet, as sparrows are easily disturbed. Leave during winter for use as a snug roost.

You will need

pencil
ruler
square
6mm/¼in medium density
 fibreboard (MDF)
tenon saw
drill
wood glue
masking tape
small metal eyelet and
 hook
self-adhesive roof flashing
craft knife
cutting mat
metal ruler
ready-mixed tile cement
palette (wide rounded)
 knife
aquarium gravel
sisal hanging-basket liner
PVA (white) glue
paintbrush
raffia
large-eyed needle
clothes pegs (pins)
diluted brown water-
 colour paint
matt varnish
varnish brush

Typical inhabitant

sparrows

1 Following the templates at the back of the book, mark and cut out all the component parts from MDF. Drill an entry hole in the front wall, and, if required, drill a small hole in the back wall for hanging.

2 Glue the base and walls together and hold in position with masking tape until dry. Screw in an eyelet 1cm/½in from the top back corner of the right-hand wall.

3 Cut a strip of roof flashing 13cm/5in wide to fit the roof ridge. Position the roof pieces side by side, leaving enough of a gap to allow the roof to hinge open. Remove the backing and cover the ridge with the flashing.

4 Working on a small area at a time, spread tile cement over the house walls. Embed aquarium gravel firmly into the cement, choosing darker stones to outline the entry hole. Cover the walls completely with the tile gravel.

5 Coat the sisal with diluted PVA (white) glue and leave to dry. Cut a rectangle 28 x 14cm/11 x 5½in for the thatch and a strip 15 x 7.5cm/6 x 3in for the ridge. Stitch two rows of large cross-stitch in raffia along the sides of this strip, then glue and stitch it across the thatch.

6 Glue the thatch to the roof. Secure with clothes pegs (pins) until dry. Screw in the hook at the back of the roof, then glue the other side of the roof to the walls, securing with masking tape until dry. Wash the cement with brown watercolour and, when dry, varnish.

Woven willow feeder

Made from the supple branches of unstripped willow, this woven basket feeder will look very picturesque placed in the garden. The conical roof is packed with moss: as well as adding weight, it will provide nesting material.

1 Trim six withes (willow sticks) to a length of 23cm/9in from the butt (thick) end. Pierce the centre of three of these rods using a knife or bodkin and push the other three through them to form a cross. The rods should be arranged with the butt ends pointing in alternate directions. Push the rods together.

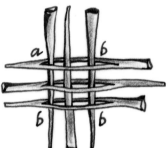

2 Insert the tips of two long withes into the slits to the left of the short rods and hold them in place by gripping the slit rods. Take one long withe in front of the three uprights, and behind the next three rods. Take the second withe behind the first three rods and in front of the next three, crossing its partner at b. Continue this weave for two complete rounds. Prise the rods apart to form the spokes of a wheel and continue weaving, keeping the weaving as tight as possible.

3 Add new weavers butt to butt or tip to tip. The new one is placed to the left of, and under, the old end, which should finish resting on a bottom rod, while the new weaver carries on over it. Join both new weavers at the same time, on neighbouring bottom rods. Weave until the base measures about 18cm/7in, finishing with tips. Secure the ends with a clothes peg (pin) and trim the bottom rods flush with the weaving.

4 Select 12 new rods. Trim the butt ends by slicing down the back of each to make a thin wedge shape. Insert each new rod to the left of a bottom rod, using a bodkin or bradawl first to loosen the weave if necessary. Using your thumb nail or a knife, make an indentation in each of the new rods where they join the base.

5 Bend each one up to form the uprights and tie them together with string at the top. Insert three weavers, tip end first, to lie to the right of three consecutive uprights. Take the left-hand weaver in front of two uprights, behind the third and out to the front again.

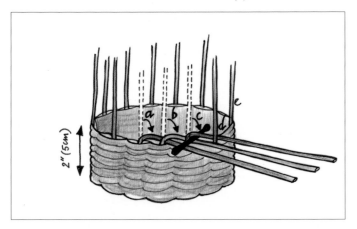

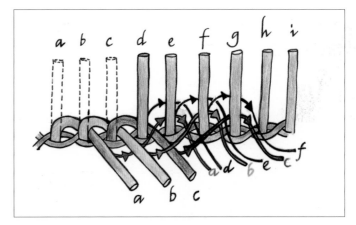

6 Repeat with the second and third. Continue this pattern, pushing the weavers down, until the side of the basket measures 5cm/2in. Join in new weavers butt to butt or tip to tip, laying the three new rods to the right of the three old rods. To finish the base of the feeder, make a kink in each upright over a pencil or pen about twice the diameter of the rod. Following the diagram, bend the first rod (a) behind the second (b) and round to the front. Bend (b) over and behind (c), then bend (c) over and behind (d) and round to the front.

7 To finish off the border: rod (a) travels in front of (c) and (d) and behind (e) and lies in front. (d) bends down and lies beside and to the right of (a). Rod (b) travels in front of (d) and (e) and behind (f) and lies in front. (e) bends over and lies beside and to the right of (b). Rod (c) travels in front of (e) and (f) and behind (g) and lies to the front. Rod (f) lies down beside and to the right of (c). There are now 3 pairs of rods (ad), (be) and (cf). Continue the work always with three pairs of rods until the end of the border. Always start with the far left pair of rods (ad) but use the right hand rod (d), (e) and (f) and make each rod do the same journey (in front of two uprights, behind one) and pull down the next upright (g), (h) and (i), until there is only one upright left.

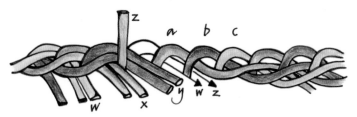

8 To finish the border, starting with the far left pair as before, each right-hand rod goes in front of two rods (which are not now upright) and behind the third, coming out through the original "arches" made with a, b and c. Pull all the rods well down into place, lying tightly together. Trim the ends neatly all round the basket.

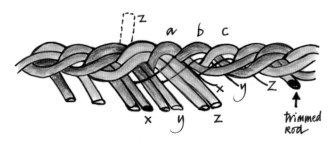

9 To make the frame for the roof, select 12 rods and trim them to 30cm/12in. Tie them securely together, 5cm/2in from the tips, using ivy. The ivy can be stripped of its leaves, or you can preserve the leaves by soaking them in glycerine, diluted half and half with water, for several days. Bend a withe into a circle a little larger than the basket. To secure the rods for the roof to the circular frame, take two long ivy stems, stripped of leaves, and tie them to the left of an upright. Wind one length around the upright above the frame and the other around the upright below the frame. Take both pieces around the frame to cross between the first and second uprights, then around the frame again to the second upright and repeat the pattern. Weave the roof using the same pattern as for the side of the basket using two sets of three rods, then change to a pairing weave, going in front of one upright and behind the next. Near the top, use a single rod weaving in and out and go as high as you can. Stuff the roof with moss.

10 To hold the moss in place, tie garden twine across the base of the roof, connecting each upright with the ones on the opposite side to make a star pattern. Cut four rods 20cm/8in long and trim both ends of each into flat wedges. Push them, equally spaced, into the weave of the roof and into corresponding positions in the basket, using a bodkin to open the weave if necessary.

Nesty nook

This cosy home, made to imitate a wren's nest, is formed from plastic-coated chicken wire covered with moss. Place the nest in a hidden position, low down in thick undergrowth or even in the bank of a stream beneath overhanging roots, as long as it is dry.

You will need

chicken wire
wire cutters
large leaves
sisal hanging-basket liner
scissors
pliers
hair net
moss
sea grass string
garden wire

Typical inhabitant

wrens

1 Cut a square of chicken wire measuring about 30cm/12in. Line the chicken wire with large leaves. Cut a square of sisal basket liner to the same size and lay it on top of the leaves.

2 Fold the four corners into the centre and join the sides by twisting the cut ends of the wires together. Leave the centre open. Tuck in the wire ends to ensure that there are no sharp bits poking out that could hurt a bird.

3 Pull from the front and back of the structure to "puff" it out and create a space inside for the nest.

4 Carefully stretch a hair net over the nest, keeping the entry hole clear.

5 Stuff moss evenly between the nest and the hair net so that the chicken wire is covered completely.

6 To define the entry hole, form a ring of sea grass string and secure it by twisting garden wire around it. Wire it into position around the hole.

Swift halt

Swifts make their nests in tunnel-shaped boxes and although they will
sometimes take to vertical access holes, a horizontal entrance hole is better,
as it prevents house sparrows and starlings taking over the box.

1 Using the templates, mark and cut out all the
pieces for the box, except the front, from pine
board. Cut lengths of batten for the front and roof.
Cut a paper pattern for the entry hole at one end of
the base and cut it out using a fretsaw.

2 Glue and nail the base to the back of the box.
Glue and nail the ends in place and add the top
batten. Cut the tongue and groove board into
15cm/6in lengths and nail to the front of the box,
attaching it to the batten and the edge of the base.

3 Drill a 15mm/⅝in hole at each joint, place a
piece of scrap timber behind to help prevent
splitting, then trim the lower edge of each board in
a chevron. Drill two holes in the back for fixing to a
wall. Sand and paint the box then leave to dry.

4 Attach the two battens to the underside of the
roof (see templates). Paint the underside black.
Cover the top of the roof with strips of self-adhesive
flashing and fit the roof on to the box. Overlap the
last strip of flashing to the back of the box.

Post box

Thick wooden stakes can be hollowed out and turned into nesting boxes. They can be sited on their own or as part of a garden fence. The self-adhesive wrapping protects from rain and also prevents the wood from splitting.

1 Using a 25mm/1in bit, drill an entry hole into the side of the post 5cm/2in from the end, then drill out the end to a depth of about 15cm/6in.

2 Chisel out the end to remove the waste left after drilling.

3 Cover the end of the post with self-adhesive roof flashing. Pierce the flashing in the centre of the entry hole and cut back to the edges, then turn back the flashing inside the hole.

4 Cut out a circle of lead flashing for the lid and remove one quarter of the circle, using the template at the back of the book. Clamp the lead between two pieces of scrap wood and fold one cut edge at 90°. Fold the second edge at 90° twice, as shown.

5 Bend the lead into a cone and join the seam, squeezing the edges together with pliers. Flatten the seam neatly against the cone.

6 Attach the roof to the post using two nails, but leave one not fully nailed in so that it can be removed to give access to the box.

Chrome birdbath

The gently sloping sides of a dustbin lid (garbage can) allow smaller birds to paddle, while larger birds can have a good splash in the middle without emptying the water.
A nightlight fitted under the bath will prevent the water freezing over on winter days.

You will need

hacksaw
galvanized dustbin lid
 (garbage can)
pliers
fabric gloves
cylindrical metal cheese
 grater
round fence post to suit
 size of grater
galvanized nails
hammer

Typical inhabitants

sparrows
starlings
blackbirds
redpolls

1 Using a hacksaw, saw across the middle of the lid's handle. Bend back both sides of the severed handle using pliers.

2 Wearing protective gloves, remove the handle from the cheese grater using pliers.

3 Push the narrow end of the cheese grater on to the post and secure it with galvanized nails through the holes left by the handle rivets.

4 Squeeze the two sides of the lid handle together to insert them into the wide end of the grater. Use a night-light placed inside the grater to stop the water from freezing.

Bryony's house

Making a birdhouse is a good way to get your children interested in birds. It will be so exciting for them to see birds nesting in a house that they have decorated and designed themselves, such as this house, drawn by the little girl shown in the picture.

You will need

photocopier
drawing
clear adhesive tape
6mm/¼in and 12mm/½in
  plywood
fretsaw
V-board
drill
sandpaper
paints
paintbrushes
varnish
pencil
ruler
square
tenon saw
wood glue
nails
hammer
self-adhesive roof flashing
mirror plates
screws
screwdriver

Typical inhabitant

tits

1 Photocopy your child's drawing, reducing or enlarging it to the required size. Tape the photocopy to a sheet of 6mm/¼in plywood and cut around the outline using a fretsaw and V-board. Drill the entry hole and sand smooth. Ask the child to paint the front, then give it several coats of varnish.

2 Using the measurements on the templates at the back of the book, mark out all the components for the nesting box on 12mm/½in plywood and cut them out. Sand all the surfaces and assemble the box using wood glue and nails. Drill an entry hole in the front of the box to the same size as the one already drilled in the front.

3 Glue and nail the painted front to the box, lining up the entry holes. Assemble the roof and cover with self-adhesive flashing, allowing overlap on the higher end of the roof to attach the box. Attach the box to a wall using mirror plates.

Duck house

The ramp for this desirable duck house has horizontal struts to make sure the occupants don't slip. Post caps on each leg will protect the wood on dry land. If it is to stand in water, use timber pressure-treated with preservative.

1 Mark out and cut out all the components using the templates at the back of the book.

2 Cut the curved roof battens and arched opening using a jigsaw. Sand all the edges.

3 On a large, flat work surface, lay out two of the legs and attach the cross rail using wood glue and nails.

4 Turn the leg assembly over and attach the first curved roof batten. Repeat the process with the other two legs.

5 Connect the front and back with the two lower cross rails. These are nailed to the inner side of the legs.

6 Attach the upper side rails at both sides. These are attached to the outside of the legs.

7 Ship-lap the back and sides of the house. As it is easier to attach the ship-lap starting at the top, glue and nail the top piece in place, but do not drive these nails in fully. Only do so after the lower piece has been glued and nailed in place.

8 Ship-lap the front in the same way, securing the door sides first. Make sure that you align the door sides carefully so that you achieve a straight, clean line when the duck house is assembled.

9 Finish off the house walls by attaching the four corner pieces. Paint the house inside and out. Put in the floor, which rests in place on the cross rails.

10 Cut a piece of roofing sheet to the size given at the back of the book, and cut two strips of polystyrene (styrofoam) filler to fit the arched front and back walls. Offer up the roof, locating it centrally.

11 Attach the roof to the front and back walls, using special roofing screws and cups.

12 Make a simple ramp by joining two planks of timber decking with cross pieces. Nail an extra cross piece to the back of the ramp at the top to hook over the batten under the door.

Home decorating dispenser

This sculptural container will not only look elegant in your garden but will encourage birds to build their nests nearby. At nest-building time, keep the dispenser topped up with scraps of wool, fur, fabric, straw and even hair.

You will need

chicken wire, approxi-
    mately 25cm/10in wide
fabric gloves
wire cutters
small pliers
thin and thick garden wire
plastic picnic plate
bradawl
coffee jar (can) lid
epoxy resin glue
large wooden bead

Typical visitors

goldfinches
sparrows
hummingbirds

1 Cut a rectangular piece of chicken wire and roll it into a cylinder. Join the wire along the edges by twisting the cut ends together. Using pliers, pull the bottom of the cylinder to draw the wires together into a tight band.

2 A third of the way from the top, form a neck by squeezing the wires together with the pliers. To create the belly of the container, pull the holes further open to fatten out the shape.

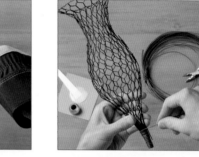

3 Splay out the rim of the container at the top. Bind the bottom with thin green garden wire. Secure both ends of the wire.

4 Attach four lengths of thicker wire, evenly spaced, around the rim of the container.

5 Make corresponding holes around the edge of a plastic plate using a heated bradawl. Thread the plate, upside down, on to the wires. Glue a coffee jar (can) lid to the plate to make a food or water container.

6 Connect the four wires to a single wire threaded with a large bead. Twist the wires neatly into position.

Scallop shelter

This little nest is made of papier-mâché. It is easily replaced each season, though the chicken wire container will last longer. Attach it to the wall with two cup hooks, in a dry place under the eaves. The scallop shell is purely decorative.

1 Tear the newspaper into small squares and soak it in water. Cover one half of a plastic bowl with a layer of wet, unpasted pieces of paper.

2 Brush paste liberally over the first layer and add more pieces, pasting each layer, until you have built up about six layers. Leave to dry in a warm place such as an airing cupboard.

3 When the papier mâché is completely dry, remove it from the plastic bowl and trim the rough edges to make a neat half-bowl shape. Cut out a semicircle of corrugated cardboard to make the backing for the nest.

4 Attach the cardboard with masking tape, then reinforce it by adding a few layers of pasted paper over the back and edges. Leave to dry.

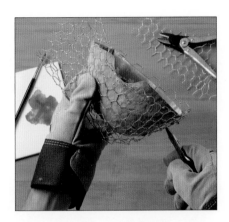

5 Paint the nest in variegated muddy
tones. Cut a piece of chicken wire,
wrap it around the nest and join the
wire ends together at the sides.

6 Squeeze the chicken wire with the
pliers to make it fit the form. Drill
two small holes in the top of the scallop
shell and one at the bottom, and wire it
on to the frame.

Willow stick nest

Half coconuts are just the right shape and size to make snug roosts for travel-weary birds. Two halves are wedged into a bunch of withes (willow sticks), and a woven sea grass wall completes the nest. To erect, stick it into the ground wherever you want it.

You will need

about 15 withes (willow sticks)
straight stick or bamboo pole
wooden napkin ring
coconut
saw
knife
raffia
sea grass string
scissors

Typical inhabitant

wrens

1 Soak the withes (willow sticks) overnight to make them pliable. Wedge them around a stick using a napkin ring. Saw a coconut in half and scrape out the contents. Using raffia, tie the withes together at the top.

2 Insert the coconut halves. Starting by the rim of the lower coconut half, weave sea grass string around the withes for three rounds.

3 Create a gap by doubling the string back on itself and changing the direction of the weaving for about four rounds.

4 Complete the weaving with three more rounds. Wedge the top of the coconut into position above the weaving and secure it by re-tying the withes at the top if necessary.

Hollow log nesting box

Choose a log you like the look of and, depending on its size, you can adapt it to suit the type of bird you want to attract to it. Mossy logs look good, as do chunks of silver birch. Avoid pieces of wood with knots or branches, as they are difficult to split neatly.

You will need

2 logs
pencil
ruler
chisel
mallet
drill
saw
hammer
nails
garden wire
scissors
pliers

Typical inhabitants

starlings
woodpeckers

1 Mark out a square on the end of one log and use a chisel and mallet to split off the first side, making sure that you work evenly along the line.

2 Repeat to remove all four sides of the square. Drill an entry hole through one of the sides.

3 Saw a 20mm/¾in slice off one end of the centre of the log.

4 Using this piece as the base of the nesting box, reassemble the log and nail the four sides together.

5 Wrap a length of garden wire around the top of the box, twist the ends to tighten it and hold the sides securely together.

6 Split the second log to make a roof for the nesting box. Attach it using one long nail, so that the roof can swivel open.

Rock-a-bye birdie box

Made to suit acrobatic birds, this box is constructed from plywood, and the removable roof is covered with flashing. The box hangs on string, though if you have a problem with predators it would be safer to use greased wire.

1 Copy the templates at the back of the book, cut out and use to mark out the shapes for the base and roof on thin plywood. Drill an entry hole in one side of the roof and sand the edges so they are smooth.

2 Cut out the plywood shapes for the base and roof using a fretsaw and V-board. Next, cut the D-shaped moulding into 10cm/4in lengths for the base and 15cm/6in lengths for the roof.

3 Glue and nail the lengths of moulding around the base, flat side outwards, starting with the central strip and working out.

4 Make a simple template to the width of the box from a piece of scrap wood and use to space the sides of the roof. Attach the roof slats as before, allowing for an overlap on each side.

5 Mark a line around the base, about 6mm/¼in below the top edge of the sides, and trim back the mouldings to this level to allow the roof to overlap the base. Varnish the box.

6 Cut a strip of 15cm/6in-wide roof flashing that is long enough to cover the roof, and smooth it over the moulding strips. Hammer the surface if you wish. Attach a length of string for hanging.

Kitchen garden bird table

This original bird table uses cooking and cleaning equipment in ingenious ways, and makes an offbeat sculpture at the same time. The sieves allow rain to drain away, and the finial is the head of a balloon whisk, into which a fat ball can be inserted.

You will need

clamps
metal sieves
wooden block
scrap wood
fabric gloves
broom handle
nails
hammer
galvanized bucket
beach pebbles
wooden spoons
sandpaper
balloon whisk
hacksaw or wire cutters
galvanized wire

Typical visitors

doves
starlings
thrushes
jays

1 Clamp the sieve handles under a wooden block and bend them through 90°. Bend them further by hand to fit around the broom handle.

2 Nail a piece of scrap wood to the bottom of the broom handle and firmly anchor this in the bucket using large beach pebbles.

3 Position the sieves along the length of the broom handle and hold each one in place by threading a wooden spoon into the bent handle. Once you are happy with the arrangement, sand grooves into the broom for the spoons to fit into.

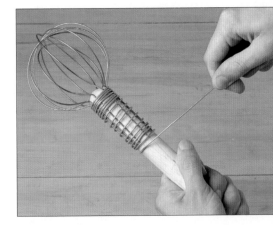

4 Using either a hacksaw or wire cutters, remove the handle of a balloon whisk and attach it to the top of the broom handle using a length of galvanized wire. This provides the perfect holder for a fat ball.

Templates

Each template gives specific dimensions for the project, and it is important to adhere to these. Enlarge on a photocopier by 400%, or trace the design and draw a grid of evenly spaced squares on your tracing. Draw a larger grid on another piece of paper and copy the design outline exactly.

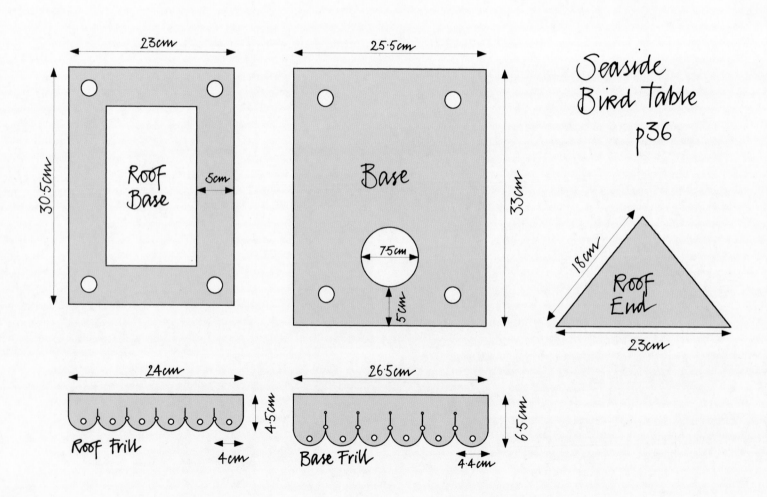

23cm

30.5cm

Roof
Base

5cm

25.5cm

Base

33cm

7.5cm

5cm

Seaside
Bird Table
p36

18cm

Roof
End

23cm

24cm

Roof Frill

4.5cm

4cm

26.5cm

Base Frill

6.5cm

4.4cm

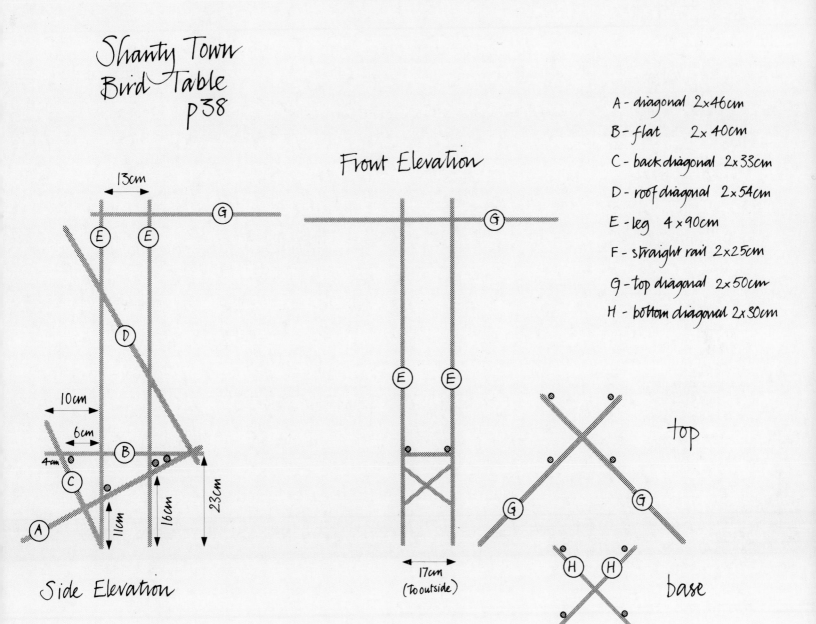

Shanty Town
Bird Table
p38

Front Elevation

A - diagonal 2×46cm

B - flat 2×40cm

C - back diagonal 2×33cm

D - roof diagonal 2×54cm

E - leg 4×90cm

F - straight rail 2×25cm

G - top diagonal 2×50cm

H - bottom diagonal 2×30cm

13cm

G

E E

D

10cm

6cm

4cm

B

C

A

11cm

16cm

23cm

Side Elevation

G

E E

17cm
(To outside)

top

G G

H H

base

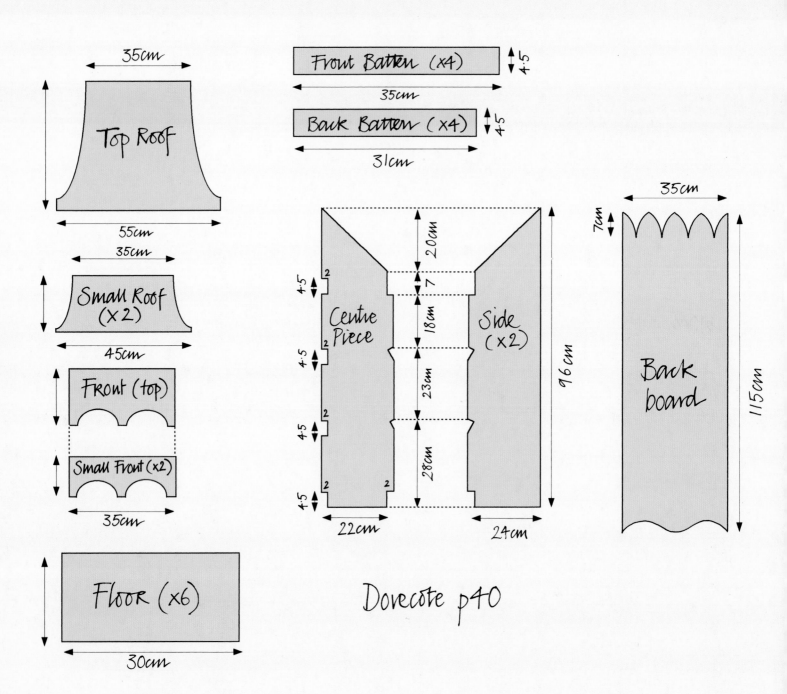

35cm

Top Roof

55cm

Front Batten (x4)

4·5

35cm

Back Batten (x4)

4·5

31cm

35cm

Small Roof
(x2)

45cm

35cm

Front (top)

Small Front (x2)

35cm

Floor (x6)

30cm

20cm

4·5   2

7

Centre
Piece

Side
(x2)

4·5   2

18cm

23cm

96cm

4·5   2

28cm

4·5   2   2

22cm

24cm

Dovecote p40

35cm

7cm

Back
board

115cm

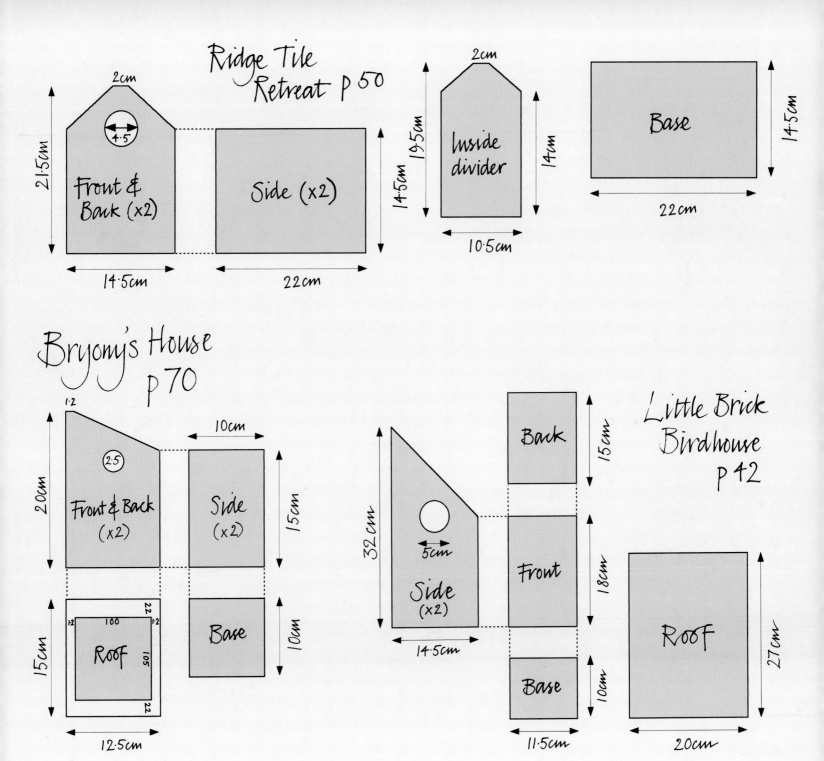

Ridge Tile
Retreat p 50

2cm

4·5

Front &
Back (x2)

21·5cm

14·5cm

Side (x2)

14·5cm

22cm

2cm

Inside
divider

19·5cm

14cm

10·5cm

Base

14·5cm

22cm

Bryony's House
p 70

1·2

2·5

Front & Back
(x2)

20cm

12·5cm

10cm

Side
(x2)

15cm

Base

10cm

15cm

Roof

1·2   100   1·2

22

105

22

Little Brick
Birdhouse
p 42

32 cm

5cm

Side
(x2)

14·5cm

Back

15cm

Front

18cm

Base

10cm

11·5cm

Roof

27cm

20cm

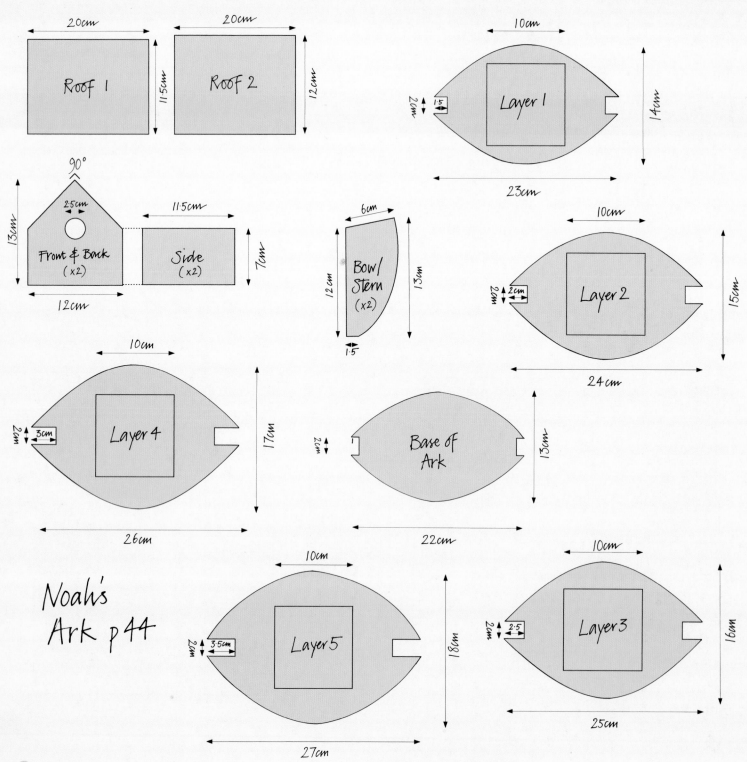

Roof 1

20cm · 11·5cm

Roof 2

20cm · 12cm

90°

Front & Back (x2)

13cm · 2·5cm · 12cm

Side (x2)

11·5cm · 7cm

Bow/ Stern (x2)

6cm · 12cm · 13cm · 1·5

Layer 1

10cm · 2cm · 1·5 · 14cm · 23cm

Layer 2

10cm · 2cm · 2cm · 15cm · 24cm

Layer 4

10cm · 2cm · 3cm · 17cm · 26cm

Base of Ark

2cm · 13cm · 22cm

Layer 5

10cm · 2cm · 3·5cm · 18cm · 27cm

Layer 3

10cm · 2cm · 2·5 · 16cm · 25cm

Noah's Ark p44

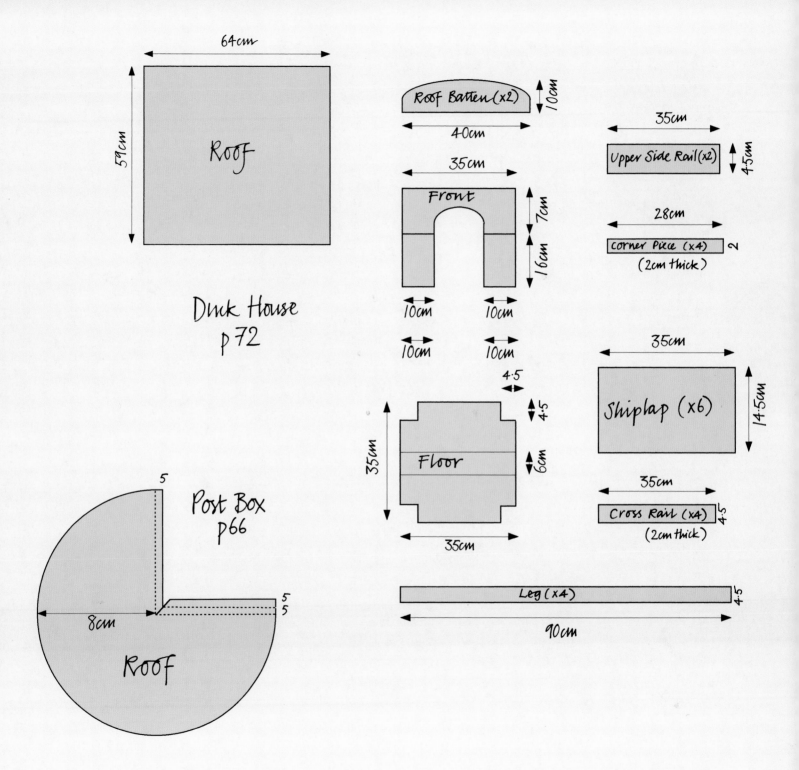

Roof

64cm

59cm

**Duck House
p 72**

Roof Batten (x2)

10cm

40cm

35cm

Front

7cm

16cm

10cm   10cm

10cm   10cm

4·5

4·5

4·5

Floor

35cm

6cm

35cm

35cm

Upper Side Rail (x2)

4·5cm

28cm

Corner Piece (x4)

2

(2cm thick)

35cm

Shiplap (x6)

14·5cm

35cm

Cross Rail (x4)

4·5

(2cm thick)

Leg (x4)

4·5

90cm

**Post Box
p66**

5

8cm

5
5

Roof

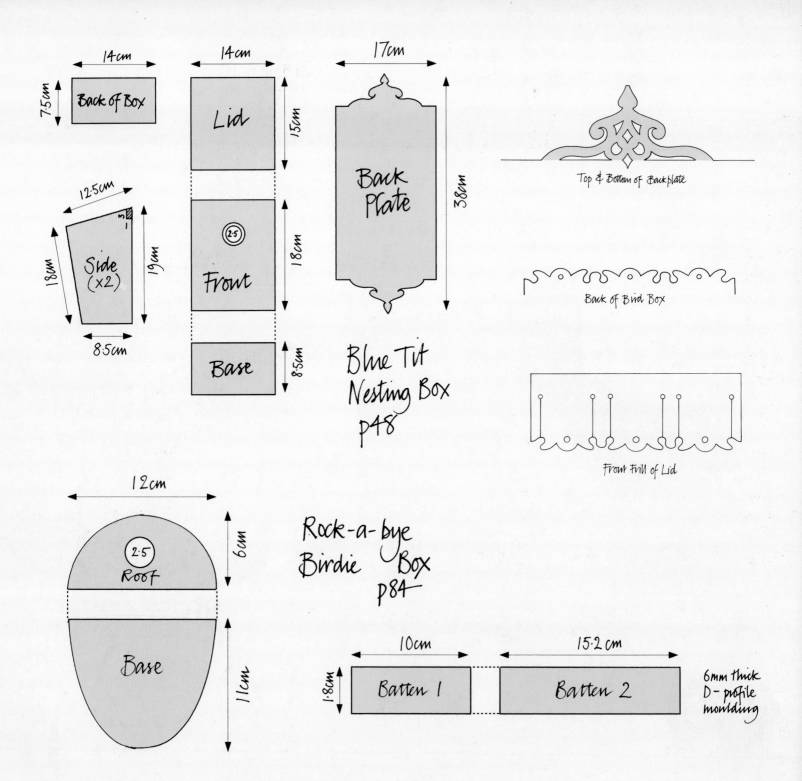

14cm

Back of Box

7.5cm

14cm

Lid

15cm

2.5

Front

18cm

Base

8.5cm

12.5cm

Side
(x2)

18cm

19cm

8.5cm

17cm

Back
Plate

38cm

Top & Bottom of Backplate

Back of Bird Box

Front Frill of Lid

Blue Tit
Nesting Box
p48

12cm

2.5
Roof

6cm

Base

11cm

Rock-a-bye
Birdie Box
p84

10cm

Batten 1

1.8cm

15.2cm

Batten 2

6mm thick
D-profile
moulding

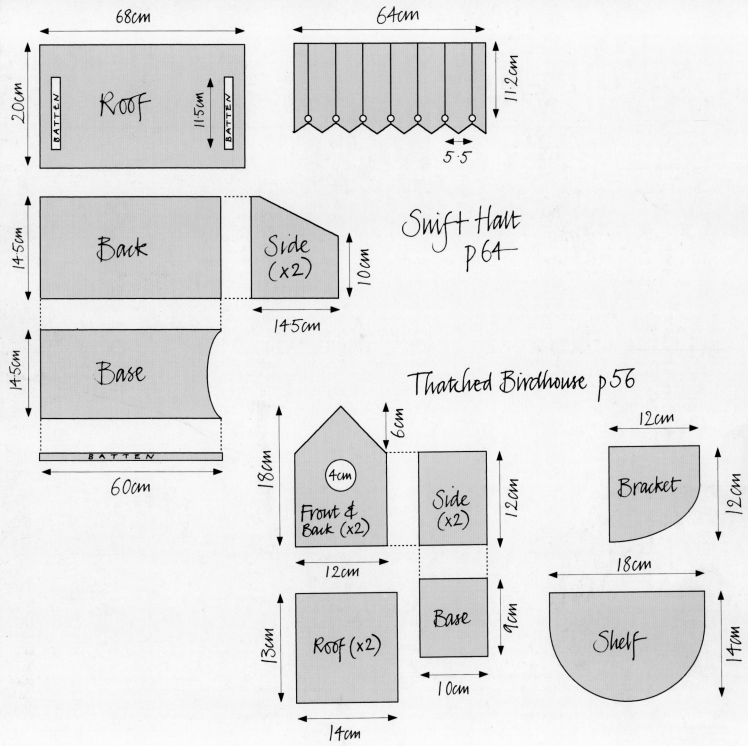

68cm

Roof

20cm

BATTEN   BATTEN

11·5cm

64cm

11·2cm

5·5

14·5cm

Back

Side
(x2)

10cm

14·5cm

Base

14·5cm

60cm

BATTEN

Swift Halt
p64

Thatched Birdhouse p56

18cm

6cm

4cm

Front &
Back (x2)

12cm

Side
(x2)

12cm

13cm

Roof (x2)

Base

9cm

14cm

10cm

12cm

Bracket

12cm

18cm

Shelf

14cm

Index

alpine house, 30
seaside bird table, 36–7
attracting birds, 12–3

barn owls, 8
baths, 13
  chrome birdbath, 68–9
bees, 9
Berlepsch, Baron von, 8
berries, 9
bird song, 10
bird tables, 12
  modern bird table, 86–7
  seaside bird table, 36–7
  shanty town bird table, 38–9
birdbaths, 13
  chrome birdbath, 68–9
birdhouses, 13
  alpine house, 30
  Bryony's house, 70–1
  clay pot roost, 34–5
  decorating, 30–3
  duck house, 72–5
  leafy birdhouse, 31
  little brick birdhouse, 42–3
  nest-in-a-boot, 52–3
  Noah's ark, 44–7
  ridge tile retreat, 50–1
  robin's log cabin, 54–5
  Shaker-style house, 31
  shell house, 32
  sites, 14
  thatched birdhouse, 56–7
birdwatching, 10–11
blackbirds, 10, 13, 14
blue tits, 10
  blue tit nesting box, 48–9
boots, nest-in-a-boot, 52–3
bottle feeder, 28–9
bounty bower, 20–1
breeding, 10–11
brick birdhouse, 42–3

Bryony's house, 70–1
butterflies, 9

cats, 15
chaffinches, 10
chicks, 11
chrome birdbath, 68–9
city gardens, 9
clay pot roost, 34–5
coconuts, 15
  coconut feeder, 26–7
  willow stick nest, 80–1
crows, 14

displays, 10
doves:
  collared doves, 10
  wall-mounted dovecote, 40–1
duck house, 72–5
dunnocks, 10

eggs, 11
elder, 9
equipment, 18–19

feathers:
  bathing, 13
  moulting, 11
  preening, 10
feeders, 12, 14
  bottle feeder, 28–9
  bounty bower, 20–1
  coconut feeder, 26–7
  sweet treat, a, 24–5
  wire bird feeder, 22–3
  woven willow feeder, 58–61
  see also bird tables
feeding birds, 10, 14–15
fighting, 10
finches, 14
flowers, 9
flying, 11

gardens, 9
greenfinches, 10
gulls, 14

hatching, 11
hawthorn, 9
hedges, 9
history, 8
hollow log nesting box, 82–3
home decorating dispenser, 76–7
house martins, 8
house sparrows, 9, 10

insects, 9

jackdaws, 8

lawns, 9
leafy birdhouse, 31
little brick birdhouse, 42–3
log cabin, robin's, 54–5
logs, hollow log nesting
  box, 82–3

magpies, 10
martins, 8, 11
  swift halt, 64–5
materials, 16–17
migrating birds, 10, 11
modern bird table, 86–7

moss:
  nesty nook, 62–3
  woven willow feeder, 58–61
moths, 9

Native Americans, 8
nest-in-a-boot, 52–3
nesting boxes, 12–13
  blue tit nesting box, 48–9
  Bryony's house, 70–1
  duck house, 72–5
  hollow log nesting box, 82–3
  nest-in-a-boot, 52–3
  nesty nook, 62–3
  post box, 66–7
  robin's log cabin, 54–5
  rock-a-bye birdie box, 84–5
  scallop shelter, 78–9
  sites, 14
  swift halt, 64–5
  thatched birdhouse, 56–7
  willow stick nest, 80–1
nests, 10–11
Noah's ark, 44–7
nuts:
  sweet treat, a, 24–5

owls, 8

paint, decorating birdhouses,
  30–3
papier-mâché, scallop
  shelter, 78–9
pigeons, 8, 9, 13
plants, 9
post box, 66–7
purple martins, 8

ridge tile retreat, 50–1
robins, 10, 14
  robin's log cabin, 54–5
rock-a-bye birdie box, 84–5

roosts, 13, 14
  clay pot roost, 34–5
  wall-mounted dovecote, 40–1

scallop shelter, 78–9
seeds:
  bounty bower, 20–1
  sweet treat, a, 24–5
Shaker-style house, 31
shanty bird table, 38–9
shells:
  scallop shelter, 78–9
  shell house, 32
sparrows, 9, 10
  thatched birdhouse, 56–7
starlings, 10, 11, 14
  ridge tile retreat, 50–1
sweet treat, a, 24–5
swift halt, 64–5

templates, 88–95
territories, 10
thatched birdhouse, 56–7
thrushes, 10
tiles, ridge tile retreat, 50–1
tits, 10, 14
  blue tit nesting box, 48–9
  rock-a-bye birdie box, 84–5
tree sparrows, 10

water, 13
Waterton, Charles, 8
White, Gilbert, 8
willow:
  willow stick nest, 80–1
  woven willow feeder, 58–61
wire bird feeder, 22–3
wood, 12, 16
woodpeckers, 8, 11, 14
woven willow feeder, 58–61
wrens, 10, 11, 14
  nesty nook, 62-3

Acknowledgements

The author and publishers would like to thank Mary Maguire for making the Bounty bower p20, Wire bird feeder p22, A sweet treat p24, Coconut feeder p26, Bottle feeder p28, Decorating birdhouses p30, Little brick birdhouse p42, Nest-in-a-boot p52, Thatched birdhouse p56, Bryony's house p70, Home decorating dispenser p76; Vicky Hurst for the Clay pot roost p34; Clare Andrews for the Seaside bird table p36 and Blue tit nesting box p48; Andrew Gillmore for the Shanty town bird table p38, Wall-mounted dovecote p40, Noah's ark p44, Ridge tile retreat p50, Robin's log cabin p54, Nesty nook p62, Swift halt p64, Post box p66, Chrome birdbath p68, Duck house p72, Willow stick nest p80, Hollow log nesting box p82, Rock-a-bye birdie box p84, Kitchen garden bird table p86; and Sandy Spalton for the Woven willow feeder p58.

Author's acknowledgements

Grateful thanks to Rupert Skinner for excellent hand modelling, Andrew Gillmore for all his help and input on the creative projects, Peter Williams for the wonderful photography and Gilly Sutton for kindly allowing us to use her garden. Also thanks to John Peterson at Riverwood for the loan of the thatched cottage on p8, and to the British Ornithological Society for invaluable information.

Picture credits:

Bruce Coleman Collection p10, FLPA p7, p11, 12, 13b and 15, Garden and Wildlife Matters Photo Library p9, and The Garden Picture Library p14.